>> CODE POWER: A TEEN PROGRAMMER'S GUIDE™

GETTING TO KNOW
Arduino

HEATHER MOORE NIVER

rosen publishing's
rosen
central®

NEW YORK

Published in 2015 by The Rosen Publishing Group, Inc.
29 East 21st Street, New York, NY 10010

First Edition

Library of Congress Cataloging-in-Publication Data

Niver, Heather Moore.
Getting to know Arduino/Heather Moore Niver.—First edition.
    pages cm--Code power : a teen programmer's guide)
Audience: Grades 5 to 8.
Includes bibliographical references and index.
ISBN 978-1-4777-7499-1 (library bound)—ISBN 978-1-4777-7501-1 (pbk.)—ISBN 978-1-4777-7502-8 (6-pack)
1. Arduino (Programmable controller)--Juvenile literature, I. Title.
TJ223.P76N58 2015
629.8'9551--dc23

                                                            2013038943

Manufactured in the United States of America

{ CONTENTS

{ INTROD

*M*ake magazine calls Arduino "the little microcontroller that launched a maker revolution." Arduino is a combination of hardware and software that lets users do so many things, from simply making a light flash to alerting Twitter followers when fresh, hot muffins are being pulled out of the oven of a local bakery.

Arduino's Web site (http://www.arduino.cc) defines the product pretty well: "Arduino is an open-source electronics pro-totyping platform based on flexible, easy-to-use hardware and software. It's intended for artists, designers, hobbyists, and any-one interested in creating interactive objects or environments."

Unlike a computer, Arduino receives input from all kinds of sensors, so it can react to the things around it. It can also change its surroundings by controlling things like lights. Arduinos have a microcontroller on the board, which is programmed using the Arduino programming language (based on Wiring) and the Arduino development environment (based on Processing).

Arduino can work solo or it can work with a computer, which lets the computer access and react to sensor data from its sur-roundings. It can also work with other Arduinos, electronics,

>> Success can be simple and satisfying! Getting a little red light to glow is one of the first projects many Arduino users attempt.

or chips. Really, Arduino can work with almost anything. One cool example is a mood lamp that recognizes and changes light color based on facial expressions. The project uses the Arduino Duemilanove.

One of the major reasons why Arduino is such a hit is that it is an open-source programmable controller. The plans are all available for free online with the click of a mouse. Users can put others' plans to use, and then they can change them however they want. They can even share their new creations and plans with others, as long as they follow Arduino's open-source policy.

In 2010, there were fifteen million hits to the Arduino site each month, according to Massimo Banzi, one of Arduino's creators. That's six hundred thousand in a single day! Banzi thinks that Arduino has a bright future. It might get even simpler to use, while continuing to expand and reach a broader audience. He thinks its database could get ten or even twenty times bigger, until it is even too big for a network. But Arduino's success depends on continuing to make new hardware and constant feedback that includes changes and suggestions for upgrades. In ten years, he muses, will there be an Arduino computer? Maybe.

Meanwhile, there are plenty of Arduino boards, kits, and shields to keep curious, creative tinkerers busy. Arduino is great for beginners who want simple projects and easy-to-follow instructions. But the more adventurous can build their own Arduino or change and adapt existing projects and plans. The Arduino LilyPad offers wearable options for those interested in computerized fashion, and the Arduino Robot is an Arduino on wheels ready to roll for anyone hankering for a mobile project. Arduino offers lots more possibilities, too. Read on to learn more about this creativity-inspiring microcontroller.

CHAPTER 1

BUILDING RADICAL ROBOTS AND GROOVY GADGETS

C alling all kids who ever got bored with their toys when they were young and started taking them apart: Arduino has arrived, and it's a tinkerer's dream. To most people, Arduino is a little computer that can be programmed to do really cool things using lights, sensors, and motors. Arduino is pretty easy to use, doesn't cost very much, and comes ready to customize so users can start making fantastic creations right away. Users can jump right into the world of electronics.

>> Holiday lights and music can make your home the most festive house on the block with the help of the Arduino Mega controller.

This nifty microprocessor links computers to the world around them. With the right design, plenty of hardware and software is able to interact with the physical world. The term for this is "physical computing," which involves a kind of interactive design that concentrates on the relationship between users and digital objects.

Arduino includes both hardware and software designs and can make computers respond to and control the physical world. The Arduino platform also includes wearables, which are small computers that can be worn inside of or on clothing. Wearables are traditionally part of the physical world but become part of the digital world as well through the use of electronics. Also, while being part of physical computing, they are also considered interactive art and design.

HARDWARE AND SOFTWARE, BOARDS AND SHIELDS

The name "Arduino" refers to both the product's hardware and software. Arduino hardware is the board itself, or the physical microcontroller unit. Users also need software to program the board, in order to get Arduino to perform the fun and imaginative projects they dream up. When Arduino users, known as the Arduino community, refer to a sketch, they mean a grouping of the programming source code that gives Arduino its instructions and controls how it works. Sketches are created on a computer using the Arduino integrated development environment (IDE). Users write and edit code with the IDE. Then they translate code into directions that Arduino hardware can understand. The IDE also helps move the commands from the computer to the Arduino board, a process that is known as uploading.

The written code goes into action on the Arduino board. Components are attached to the board, which controls and reacts to electricity. There are two kinds of components: sensors and actuators. Sensors, which include buttons and switches, change parts of the physical world into electricity for the board to "feel" by reacting to things like temperature, light, and motion. Actuators are mechanisms that use electricity from the board to make stuff happen. Lights, LEDs, and speakers are all examples of actuators. Most boards have a USB connector to provide power.

Arduino boards come in all shapes and sizes for all kinds of projects. The Arduino Mini and Pro Mini are as tiny as postage stamps. Bigger boards such as the Arduino Mega have a lot more power and options for connecting. The round LilyPad is made for wearable applications, whereas the

>> The circular Arduino LilyPad is designed to attach to fabrics. It can be used to make eye-catching clothes, such as a skirt that blinks LED lights with each movement.

Fio works for wireless creations. Projects that run on batteries often make use of the Arduino Pro.

Arduino shields add extra options to a general Arduino board. They can do almost anything anyone can imagine. Some say that shields may be the reason why Arduino is so popular. A shield fits onto the Arduino board. Usually, shields pass through these connections into another row of header sockets, so users can make stacks of shields over an Arduino base at the bottom. Arduino shields include the Arduino GSM, Ethernet, WiFi, Wireless SD, Motor, Wireless Photo, and Proto.

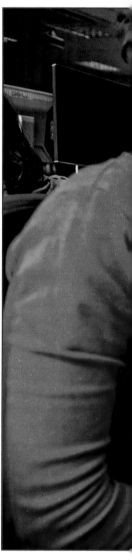

POSSIBILITIES IN PROGRAMMING

Computers are amazing machines, but without programs, they would just be expensive boxes of wires and chips. Computer programs tell the computer what to do or give it step-by-step instructions to follow to get certain results. Computer programmers achieve this by using code to write software programs.

Programming uses many unique languages. The Arduino programming language is based on C. Lots of people communicate in more than one language, so programming languages can be thought of as just another way to communicate. Luckily, programming languages have a much smaller vocabulary, and it's written not spoken. Users who are already familiar with any other programming language will find it easy to get the hang of C.

>> Computer science students at Aberystwyth University in Wales learn to program the LilyPad. It is easy for anyone who is already familiar with other programming languages to learn Arduino's

It's easy to get started with Arduino, but anyone who wants to learn more about the technical aspects can learn more about the language on which Arduino is based, which is called AVR C. This code can easily be added to Arduino programs.

NEARLY INVISIBLE: EMBEDDED SYSTEMS

Although it's no easy task to define an embedded system, it's a lot like its name implies. It's a system embedded, or inserted, into a larger device to make something happen. Embedded systems control, monitor, or assist the operation of gears, equipment, or a factory. Users may hardly know embedded systems are there. These devices are designed to perform a very specific purpose. In short, an embedded system is any computing system that is not a basic computer with a monitor and keyboard. Instead of being controlled by a keyboard or a mouse, like a traditional computer, an embedded system is controlled with switches and foot pedals, for example.

Lots of embedded systems are constantly reacting and responding to the environment around them. This is why they are often used in a car's antilock braking system. Embedded systems can react faster than a human, so in the braking system, the car can brake faster than the driver's foot. Another good example is an air conditioner. When we want our houses to cool down on a hot summer afternoon, the air conditioner's microcontroller keeps track of the temperature and humidity in the building. A microcontroller measures the qualities of the air and knows when to trigger a servo that lets fresh air in or pulls moisture out.

MICROCONTROLLERS AND MORE

Embedded systems are made up of three parts: sensors, microcontrollers, and outputs. Sensors are what measure the conditions in the area around them, like temperature, light, pressure, and even motion. The brain of the embedded system is a mini computer called a microcontroller. A microcontroller, such as Arduino, has a processor and a memory, so programs run right on it. Output devices are what affect the surroundings. Also known as actuators, examples of output devices include light-emitting diodes (LEDs) and servo motors.

The microcontroller is really made up of a tiny computer on a chip. On an Arduino board, the chip has twenty-eight pins that are fitted into a socket in the middle of the board. This is where the memory processor and electronics are found. Microcontrollers have input/output pins that control the attached electronics. Arduino is a ready-made microcontroller board that lets users skip over the complicated and sometimes confusing process of programming a microcontroller. Learning to do this could take a lot of time and patience. The Arduino microcontroller platform is programmed with a Universal Serial Bus (USB) cable.

DO YOU ARDUINO?

Who uses Arduino? Designers do. Engineers do. Soon, maybe you will, too. Just about everyone is realizing how cool this little microprocessor can be. Even some bakers use Arduino. BakerTweet was created so a bakery in London could alert its Twitter followers when fresh hot muffins were just coming out of the oven. Bakers just have to turn the heat- and

>> A dancer is painted with conductive ink in preparation of becoming part of a"human synthesizer," playing the music of UK composer Calvin Harris, in 2009.

flour-resistant dial to the delicious concoction that's ready to eat and press a button to send a tweet to all their followers.

Musicians use Arduino, too. Rockterscale uses a musician's movements to measure how much the crowd reacts or how hard users rock out when playing *Guitar Hero* or *Rock Band*. The BBC created this Arduino project that can also be used by live bands playing at concerts. Cool features include the Hat of Rock, which measures the amount of head thrashing by either band or audience members, and a dance floor, which measures how much people are dancing. All the sensors are gauged from zero to eleven by an Arduino-powered guitar pointer that receives all the data to measure how hard the band is rocking. When it hits eleven, the LED lights up.

>>PUNK ROCK PROGRAMMING

In his book *Arduino Wearables*, author Tony Olsson likens Arduino to punk rock music, which is known for its simple basic chords. Learn these chords, and the guitarist is ready to rock and roll: he or she can learn a song, then write a song, then start a band. Arduino is just like that. It is considered simpler than most other microcontrollers. Users can get started right away, and they don't need to be engineers or know much about electronics. The learning curve is small, and anyone can start playing around with Arduino and learn as they go.

HACKING: IT'S NOT ALWAYS A DIRTY WORD

Cybercrime seems to be in the news all the time these days. Articles detail how banks and other businesses have been "hacked," or been the victim of crime using computers illegally. But readers shouldn't be alarmed when they see references to hacking on Arduino sites. Hacking also has a much broader meaning than illegally obtaining or altering information in data systems. Hacking can also refer to changing the characteristics of a system to make it do something different than what it was made to do. Computer codes can be changed to do whatever the user wants.

>> Hackers such as those taking part in the Hacker Project Citizen competition, shown here, legally try to change, adapt, and improve code, rather than commit cybercrime.

Arduino is all about hacking. In fact, its creators count on it. The Arduino Web site even has a hacking page (http://arduino.cc/en/Hacking/HomePage) with links to instructions on how to make the most of the various Arduinos, a process that is better known on the site as "extending" Arduino. The microprocessor can be easily changed, the software can be modified with code changes, and the physical boards can be adapted to different uses by changing the circuitry.

WHAT'S HOT...AND WHAT'S NOT

Arduino is definitely a nifty gadget with a lot of potential for fun and creativity. One plus is that its software works across many platforms, meaning it is cross-platform software. Users can work with the Arduino microcontroller on Windows (PC), OS X, or Linux. Much of the other available microcontrollers' software can only run on Windows. Also, because Arduino is published as an open-source tool, the software is free and available on the Internet. One quick click and users can download software to start learning Arduino.

Yet even the coolest tech toys have their detractors. For example, not everyone is a big fan of the premade Arduino shields. Some users think it's easier and cheaper to just build their own shields. Some feel that while Arduino is easy to use, it is something "serious" programmers may find limits what they can do. Users who want a more powerful machine sometimes decide to start from the ground up and build their own microprocessors, leaving Arduino for beginners.

Even beginners might find getting information on Arduino a little challenging. Some users have a harder time putting together information on the Arduino because it's found in various locations all over the Internet. Sometimes it can be challenging to find answers.

Not every engineer is singing the praises of Arduino's accessibility either. In fact, some think that's a problem. They criticize Arduino's makers for making the process of creating products *too* easy. Some engineers argue that Arduino is filling the market with uninspiring items that don't fuel the imagination. Others are concerned that Arduino might be replacing the engineer.

CHAPTER 2

THE ORIGINS OF ARDUINO

Arduino was initially created for Italian design students who needed an inexpensive platform for their projects. These days, Arduino is used by all kinds of people: beginners who just want to make some cool creations, electronics experts who take their projects very seriously, and just about everyone in between. Arduino has exploded in popularity, and people all over the world are having a blast being creative.

NECESSITY SPARKS AN IDEA

In 2005, something exciting was about to develop at the Interaction Design Institute in the city of Ivrea, Italy. Professor Massimo Banzi was teaching electronics to university students when he met David Cuartielles, an engineer visiting from Malmö University in Sweden. Both men were feeling a little frustrated that electronics seemed to be something accessible only to engineers. They thought that design students could surely get a lot of inspiration from electronics and use electronics as an outlet for their creativity as well.

>> Massimo Banzi is one of the creators of Arduino. He and David Cuartielles wanted to create a microcontroller that was more accessible to design students.

Even before the creation of Arduino, some students used a microcontroller called BASIC Stamp. The problem was that the unit was so expensive that many students couldn't afford it. Universities sometimes purchased the microcontrollers for their students to use, but even schools could afford to buy only a certain number, which students had to share. Because the microcontrollers were in short supply, students wouldn't do their work.

Price wasn't the only problem. Even those who had the money to drop on BASIC Stamp were at a disadvantage if they didn't have a background in electronics. Additionally, the

>> BASIC Stamp microcontrollers, such as those being produced here, were expensive and hard to use unless one had a background in electronics. They also didn't have enough power for certain projects.

microcontroller simply didn't have enough power to handle the sorts of projects Banzi and Cuartielles had in mind. Finally, it didn't play nice with the Macintosh computers many students used for their projects.

Banzi and Cuartielles were determined to come up with a microcontroller that was affordable and simple to use—something they could learn to use quickly and get right to work. They wanted something that was more modern, too. They recruited programmers Tom Igoe, a teacher from New York City, and his former student David Mellis. Gianluca Martino later joined them to form the Arduino team.

HELLO WORLD! WELCOMING ARDUINO

A friend of Banzi's at the Massachusetts Institute of Technology (MIT) had developed a special programming language called Processing, which worked well with many design projects. Processing was becoming a pretty big deal because it made it easy for even the most novice programmer to create amazing graphics. What made Processing such a snap was its integrated development environment (IDE).

Banzi took notice and decided to figure out how to create this kind of software tool to code a microcontroller. A student of his, Hernando Barragán, wrote his thesis on the concept, which, in turn, resulted in the creation of a wiring platform called, appropriately enough, Wiring. The platform included an easy-to-use IDE and a ready-to-use circuit board. Banzi thought it was a great start but immediately wanted to work on simplifying the whole platform, making it cheaper and even easier to use. The result was Arduino.

By 2005 the team had the first sample board, called a prototype. They didn't want it to cost any more than dinner out at a pizza place, around $30. They also wanted to be sure it was kind of funky and cool looking, so it would stand out visually. Because many other boards were green, Arduino's was blue. Whereas other boards tried to minimize the number of pins and outputs, Arduino had plenty. Finally, Banzi added one last quirky touch: a map of Italy etched on the back of each microcontroller.

>> The Arduino team made their products a different color, added lots of pins, and etched a map of Italy on the back, as seen on this Mega controller.

Arduino was deliberately constructed from inexpensive parts that anyone could find, so that people could build their own boards from the ground up if they wanted to. BASIC Stamp and other similar boards required users to buy many more items besides the boards, which made it more expensive and more complicated. But one key approach was that they also wanted the Arduino board to be ready to use straight from the box, known as plug-and-play. Anyone could pull it from the box, plug Arduino into any computer—Mac or PC—and start to play.

OPENING UP

But their troubles weren't over yet. The Interaction Design Institute was going to close, and the men didn't want their creation to fall through the cracks when the school shut its doors. Open-source software had been around since the 1980s and really started to get noticed a decade later, when the Internet started getting popular. Open-source software can be downloaded, used, and even changed for free. This type of software and hardware combination allows users to develop and improve the product—a perfect fit for Arduino.

Banzi and Cuartielles had some trouble figuring out how to make Arduino open source. Banzi's technology had good compatibility with various operating systems, so all Cuartielles needed to do was fix some bugs in it before they could start making boards. Mellis began work on writing the software program, and after Igoe came in as adviser, Martino was able to manufacture the board.

At first friends of the designers bought Arduino, but it took off from there. The Arduino team decided their product could be useful to more than just the students at that school. Even without any kind of advertising or marketing, word of Arduino spread like wildfire. Soon the Internet community was chattering about Arduino and playing with it, too.

Phil Torrone was senior editor at *Make* magazine when he first read about Arduino. He realized that Arduino allowed people to get started on a project without having to learn everything about electronics first; they could get right to work. If a fashion designer wants to get a piece of clothing to blink and flash with lights as the wearer moves, with Arduino, he or she can get it done in just a few minutes.

Arduino hardware and software are both open source. Other people can look at a design and improve it, and then they can do whatever they want: change, expand, and experiment. They can remove parts or add them, use the new creation, and then release it back out to the public with all the credits for other people to use.

FREE FOR ALL

Obviously, when it comes to physical computing, Arduino isn't the only microcontroller or microcontroller platform on the market. The idea for Arduino itself wasn't even that original. Arduino, however, was created to be an educational tool, which meant it needed to be designed so that users could learn from the projects of previous users, and they, in turn, could share their projects for others to use. The solution was to make Arduino open source, which meant that anyone could copy, reproduce, and change it however they wanted. So while there were other similar boards on the market, Arduino was the first to be released under an open-source license.

While not so unusual with regard to software, this was a very unusual approach to hardware. Most technology companies keep information about how they make their products a closely guarded secret, in order to keep money coming in and avoid having the competition come out with a similar product. Making it open source also kept the cost of Arduino low because the makers didn't have to spend as much on new developments.

Arduino uses the open-source model to inspire innovation and creativity. It's a way to make sure other people see new designs and improve on them with the help of other users. People can sell their designs made from open-source hardware as long as they follow certain guidelines. In exchange for using the work of others, users agree to release what they create back out to the public and make it available for others to use and improve.

Open sourcing prevents the problem of standardization of patent systems where users would have to get permission to use Arduino.

>>SHARE AND SHARE ALIKE

Arduinos are sold under a Creative Commons Share-Alike (CC-SA) license. Under the CC-SA, people who use a preexisting plan can change, share, and distribute it, as long as they give the original creator credit and distribute their newly changed creation under the same CC-SA license. So with Arduino, users can make any changes they want to the original Arduino board or how it's programmed and share it with the public. They just need to make sure they release it under the same CC-SA license, giving credit to the original Arduino creators.

The patent system prevented people from learning how things worked unless they hacked it. Keeping Arduino as open-source hardware means it can be used to educate. Every invention is a new creation for the community, based on what other people have done. Arduino's model has been described as using a ladder that other people have started to build. A user changes it and then lets other people use her or his design to use the ladder or climb higher.

Of course Arduino isn't the only open-source microcontroller out there. Chumby is about the size of a clock radio and runs off software widgets that can tell us the weather or play music. Bug is another system that involves snapping modules together to make different computing devices. But Arduino is the one that users can start using and within an hour they can finish a simple

>> Chumby is an open-source microcontroller that connects to the Internet to tell the user what the weather is like, show pictures, or play music.

project, like making an LED blink. And Arduino can also be used for more sophisticated projects like the Blinkie Blanket, which uses five touch-triggered LED lights to help the user relax. This kind of blanket does more than help people ease into a nice nap: Blinkie Blanket can be useful for patients who need help controlling their breathing.

FROM ARDUINO SPRANG MAKERBOT

Zach Hoeken Smith didn't know anything about electronics when he started puttering around with Arduino in 2009, but he wasn't discouraged. Instead, he decided to figure out how to make a three-dimensional printer for his first project. Three-dimensional printing is also known as additive manufacturing. In 3-D printing, objects are made one layer at a time based on a design file. Instead of taking a larger object and removing material, such as in machining, in 3-D printing material is added.

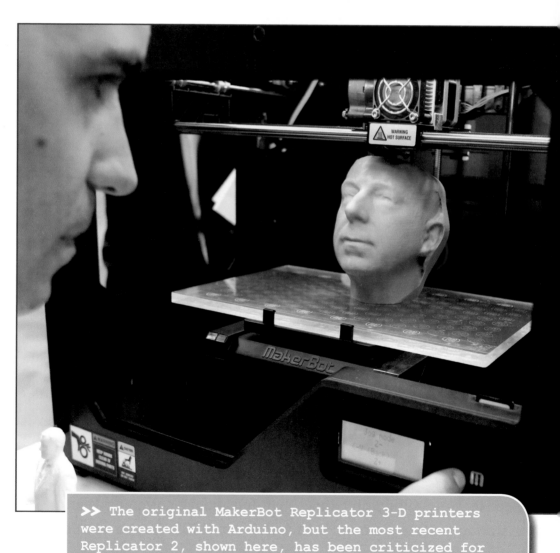

>> The original MakerBot Replicator 3-D printers were created with Arduino, but the most recent Replicator 2, shown here, has been criticized for not being an open-source product.

Smith got started by just playing around and experimenting with Arduino. The result of his experimentation was a three-dimensional desktop printer called the MakerBot 3D printer. The MakerBot prints with thin plastic threads called filament to create actual 3-D objects using multiple Arduinos. By downloading a 3-D model from the Internet or designing and scanning it into a computer, the plastic is pulled into the machine and prints out a real object that looks exactly like what the user wants. With a 3-D printer, anyone can make almost anything: a coat hook, a lemon juicer, or even an action figure with seventy different bendable joints.

CHAPTER 3

ALL ABOARD FOR ARDUINO BOARDS

Arduinos can be divided into three basic categories: boards, shields, and kits. The majority of Arduinos are boards, such as the Uno, LilyPad, and Robot, just to name a few. Arduino keeps coming out with newer, cooler, more creative, and more interesting boards all the time.

Although there are all kinds of Arduino boards of every shape and size, they all have certain things in common. They all have digital input and output pins, some of which can also work as PWM (pulse-width modulation) pins. All boards have analog input and output pins, as well as serial (or digital) communication pins. And last but, of course, not least, they all work with Arduino software.

UNPACK AND PLAY: UNO

The first Arduino was the serial Arduino, which was used only by the Arduino team and some of their friends. The first popular Arduino was called the NG, which was followed by several versions, such as the Diecimila and the 2009 Duemilanove. In 2010, Arduino released the Uno, which is the Italian word for "one." The Arduino Uno is a microcontroller board that is

>> The Arduino Uno is popular with new users because it is nearly ready to use straight out of the box. The Uno can be used to make a full-color Tetris game.

practically ready to use from the box. Just unpack from the box, connect to a computer or power source (such as an AC-to-DC adapter or simply a battery), and play. One of the beauties of the Uno is that it comes ready with everything users need to run the microcontroller.

The Uno has a USB chip that converts the USB to serial. It's a little more expensive, but it's more flexible. Sketches for older Unos work just fine on newer versions, a process that is known as backward compatibility. The Uno is also ready to use on either Mac or Windows, although Windows users do need to install a special file.

>>BREADBOARDS AND BOTS

A breadboard in the electronics world is a lot different from the one many of us use in the kitchen. Breadboards connect a temporary circuit when making experimental models. Physically, breadboards are plastic rectangular boxes with holes for inserting electronic parts and wires. Users don't have to worry about soldering wires. Wires are inserted into the holes and connected by metal lines. Breadboards make it easy to experiment and play around until the user figures out exactly what he or she wants to do. Once the user decides on a final arrangement of wires, he or she can create a more permanent form. Breadboards come in a few different sizes and can be connected to one another to develop bigger circuits.

Breadboards can also be used when making something like a robot. For example, *Popular Mechanics* magazine uses a breadboard in their Build Your First Robot design. The breadboard wires the Arduino Uno to the robot's hardware. In this case the breadboard directs electronic signals from one part of the robot to another and allows users to change the arrangement without having to solder wires. It works like a switchboard; the magazine describes Arduino as the bot's brain and the breadboard is its nervous system. For instructions and more information on how to build a robot using the Arduino Uno, go to the *Popular Mechanics* Web site "Build Your First Robot" project page (http://www.popularmechanics.com/technology/engineering/robots/build-your-first-robot).

The Uno is a pretty flexible little microcontroller. For all its good points, though, it does have some limitations. Unlike some other microcontrollers, the Uno can work only as a USB/serial port, rather than also operating as items such as a keyboard or mouse. That being said, more experienced users can adapt the Uno using a built-in chip to reprogram it to act like a keyboard, disk drive, or any USB device.

Some interesting projects can be undertaken using the Uno. For instance, it can be used as part of a project to make a "smart" trashcan. This is a wastepaper basket that senses movement and catches paper thrown into the air. The Uno can be used to control the light and heat in an entire house, going so far as to let homeowners access their heat and turn it on over the Internet. One hacker even used the Uno to design a rechargeable phone that can make calls and has a touch screen. Another musically inclined user figured out how to use the Arduino Uno to use his guitar to send e-mails. The computer typed certain letters and other keystrokes based on his chords and notes.

LOOK OUT, HERE COMES THE LEONARDO

The Leonardo is a microcontroller board that was the first Arduino to have its own USB communication. So the Leonardo can act as a mouse or keyboard to a connected computer, just with the connection of a USB cable. Another nifty feature is that the Leonardo doesn't need to be reset by pressing a button. Users can reset it using computer software.

>> The Arduino Leonardo can act like a keyboard or a mouse by connecting to a computer via a USB. The Leonardo is recommended for more advanced programmers.

Unlike the Uno, the Leonardo uses only one microcontroller to run sketches and connect to a computer with a USB. The Uno has two separate microcontrollers for these jobs. Using only one chip means it's easier for the Leonardo to communicate with the computer. The board can do both at the same time. Running the library for keyboard and mouse all the time can make it hard to program the board. One way to avoid this issue is by installing a control system like a physical switch to turn the keyboard and mouse functions on and off as needed.

When the Arduino Leonardo came out in 2012, some felt it was more a new beginning than a replacement to the Arduino

Uno. This meant new shield designs were necessary. Also, the Leonardo was not considered a good "starter" Arduino; the Uno was better for beginners. Some people felt that there was some space of the board that was wasted, with areas that would have been put to better use as space for additional user LEDs or circuitry for rechargeable batteries. Also, replacing the board's microcontroller isn't cheap.

People who want to use the Leonardo have a lot of projects from which to choose. One example of a cool use of the Leonardo is called Bleuette, the hexapod robot. It has six legs and can scuttle around on its own thanks to the power of the Leonardo and a custom shield. The Annikken Andee project uses the Leonardo to communicate with an Android smartphone without having to spend a lot of time writing code.

EXPLORE WITH THE ESPLORA

Just one look at the Arduino Esplora and it's clear that this product is meant for fun. It looks just like a controller for a video game. The Esplora was introduced in December 2012 as a handheld controller that is easy to use and does not require the user to solder or deal with breadboards. Just pull it out of the box and go. Sensors are already in place, such as a light sensor and temperature sensor, as well as a joystick, four pushbuttons, a slider, a buzzer, a microphone, and more. It can act just like a computer, mouse, or keyboard, so it can be customized for music software, 3-D modeling, or even word processing, though the possibilities hardly end there. All users need to do is write some software that takes information from the inputs and uses it to control the outputs.

Based on the Arduino Leonardo, the Esplora has features that include built-in sensors that allow the user to connect it to a computer with a USB cable and start playing. It can communicate with a computer, another Arduino, or other microcontrollers. The Esplora is programmed a bit differently than other Arduino boards since the sensors are already installed.

ROBOT...ON WHEELS

In 2013, Arduino went mobile in robotic form. The Robot is the first Arduino microcontroller on wheels. It is controlled a lot like the Leonardo. Designed in conjunction with the educational robotics team at Complubot, the Robot has two circular boards and a processor for each board; the motor board is in charge of the motors, while the control board keeps track of the sensors and figures out how to operate the unit. Each board is a full Arduino board that users can program with the Arduino IDE. Both processors have built-in USB communication.

The Robot can be powered through the USB connection. Four AA batteries can also be used, but the creators recommend using only rechargeable batteries, according to the Arduino Web site. The Robot includes a battery charger that requires external power from an AC-to-DC adapter. When the Robot is disconnected from the USB, the motors and battery charger are disabled.

The Arduino team worked with Complubot to make a robot that would teach users about robotics. It features color LCD, a microSD card slot, an EEPROM, a speaker, a compass, and a knob, plus some buttons and LEDs. It comes with connectors already soldered and prototyping areas so that users can customize it with sensors and more. The Arduino Robot comes ready to go with eleven starter projects. Although it's super cool to build a robot, some users might find the Arduino Robot pretty pricey at a suggested retail price of more than $200.

THE LOVELY LILYPAD

Arduino can be used for more than robots and phones. Leah Buechley and SparkFun Electronics designed and developed a circular board known as the LilyPad, which has big connecting pads that users can sew on clothing. Wearables and e-textiles are sewn into or on fabric with special conductive thread. As of this writing, the most recent LilyPad Main Board featured a flat back and fewer external parts to keep it as small and simple as possible. Projects can be as basic as creating a skirt with lights that blink as the wearer moves.

Arduino software can connect to a LilyPad Arduino Main Board, LilyPad Arduino Simple Board, or LilyPad Arduino Simple Snap, depending on the project the user has in mind. The LilyPad is compatible with both Windows and Mac OS X, and can be powered by connecting to a USB or other external power supply, such as an AC-to-DC adapter or battery.

Think the LilyPad is just for the fashionable? Guess again. Buechley made a handy jacket to wear while riding a bicycle called the Turn Signal Biking Jacket. Lights in the back of her jacket flash to signal when she's turning right or left just by pressing a switch located at the end of each sleeve. The user just clicks the switch again to turn them off. If she wants to be really visible at night, she can click both switches at the same time so both flashers on the back of her jacket blink.

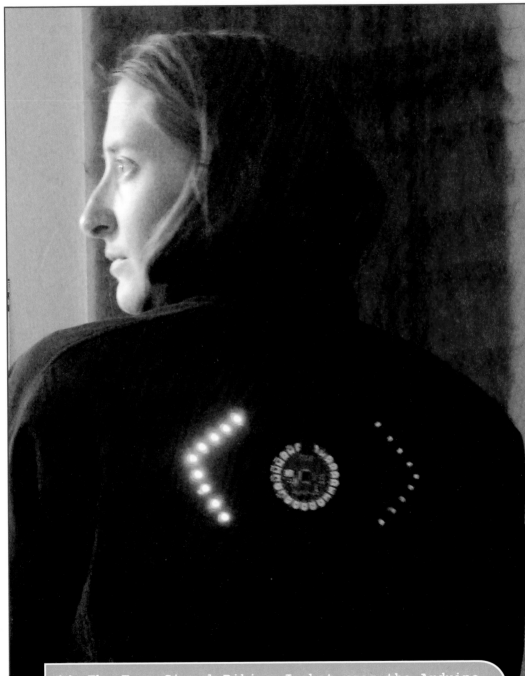

>> The Turn Signal Biking Jacket uses the Arduino LilyPad to flash lights that indicate which way the biker is turning, or simply to make the cyclist more visible at night.

LilyPad users have to be careful about a few things. Users should be aware that the LilyPad shouldn't be powered with more than 5.5 volts. They also need to avoid plugging the power in backward. Either of these actions can ruin the LilyPad. Finally, they should be sure to use only Arduino software versions 0010 or higher. Earlier versions will work, but they may be frustratingly slow and some functions will turn off. Also, clothes made with LilyPad should only be carefully washed by hand.

BLUE AND SKINNY: THE ARDUINO PRO AND PRO MINI

The little (a bit more than 2 × 2 inches [5 × 5 centimeters]) blue Arduino Pro is made to be a part of a project that might run on batteries. The Mini, of course, is smaller than the Pro at 0.7 × 1.3 inches (1.7 × 3.3 cm). Both the Pro and Mini are only .03 inch (0.8 millimeter) thick. Because both the Pro and Mini are small, they are suggested for use in projects where users don't want the board to be visible. SparkFun Electronics teamed up with Arduino to design and manufacture both boards.

One of the highlights of these boards is that their connectors are open; they do not have any on-board USB or pin headers. These are very inexpensive Arduinos, but they do take some extra work and knowledge to operate properly. (Newer users are directed to the Uno.) For those with more electronics experience—they should know about system voltage, for example—the Pro and Mini allow them to solder in connectors or wires however they want, so they have a lot of flexibility when planning their projects.

There are several versions of the Arduino Pro and Mini, each with its own voltage and clock speed. It's important to know which one you're using, as the board's power can come from a USB header, a battery, or an external power supply. An FTDI cable can also power either the Pro or Mini. External power can be supplied by soldering a power jack to the board. Some users describe the Pro Mini as a Duemilanove that lacks only a USB port and FTDI chip. The Mini has a snazzy OSHW (open source hardware) logo to add a little visual pizzazz.

If users have to put a lot of work into getting a Pro ready to use, it had better result in some cool projects, right? It doesn't disappoint. One user used a Pro Mini to adapt a model quad copter (a four-bladed helicopter). The Arduino Pro Mini took the place of the existing electronics. Although it made the copter a little on the heavy side, it still took off.

Arduino offers plenty more boards than there is space to mention here, so check out some of the nifty boards and project possibilities for Arduino USB, Simple, SimpleSnap, Micro, Nano, Fio, Mini Mega 2560, Mega ADK, and Ethernet. And who knows what Arduino will dream up for its next board?

CHAPTER 4

ARDUINO ACCESSORIES AND SHIELDS

The Arduino boards offer a lot of creative choices for projects all on their own, but there are other options to make the boards do even more. Shields make it possible to do everything from connecting Arduino to the Internet to create a working mobile phone, from making a Web server to hosting a Web site, and more. Arduino also offers other accessories that can help make any project more exciting or simply easier to construct.

SHIELDS

It has been argued that Arduino owes much of its celebrity to the great number of plug-in shields that make it fairly easy for users to add handy features to many standard Arduino boards. Basically, a shield helps an Arduino board do even more. Pretty much any imaginable project has a shield that can help make a programming dream become a reality. Not every board works with shields, but those that do can have shields mounted right on them, connected by the pins. Once the shield is connected, the Arduino may be able to do more things, such as control various devices or get more information.

It's simple to stack shields, but it's important to make sure they're all compatible with one another. Also, no two shields should use the same pin. Some shields avoid this issue by using a jumper to add more options to assigning pins. Shields with display-like features probably won't pass through this way. For those who are unsure about which shields use which pins, they can visit http://shieldlist.org.

>> Arduino shields can be stacked to add more options and make projects even more exciting. But it's important to make sure the shields are compatible with one another before stacking.

Most shields are developed to use with the Arduino Uno, but the Mega and the Leonardo might be used with certain shields, too. New shields are created all the time, and of course, since they're Arduino, the hardware, software, and all documentation is free and open source.

But Arduino isn't the only source for shields. XBee is just one of many other shields out there ready to make the most of any Arduino project. The XBee shield can make an Arduino project wireless.

GET GOING WITH THE GSM SHIELD

One way to harness the Internet is with Arduino's GSM shield. It can connect users to the Internet with a wireless network in a few simple steps. Just plug the GSM shield into Arduino and connect a SIM card from an operator offering general packet rating service (GPRS) coverage. In just a few easy steps, the Internet is accessible.

The GSM shield includes several LED lights to let users know what's going on. The "on" light is illuminated to show that the shield has power. "Status" lights up to indicate when the modem is powered up and when data is transferring to or from the GSM/GPRS network. Finally, "net" flashes when it's communicating with the radio network.

The GSM also has the ability to make and receive voice calls with the help of an external speaker and microphone circuit, as well as send and receive text messages. Users cannot make and receive calls from the public Internet, but the Bluevia SIM card that comes with the GSM can take incoming requests on the Bluevia network.

One doctoral student at the Massachusetts Institute of Technology dreamed up and developed a sturdy, working cell phone using the hardware and software of the GSM shield as well as the library. The DIY Cellphone is another open-source project, and with some soldering experience, almost anyone can make it. It's far from a smartphone, but its features include an LED screen, as well as the ability to send and receive phone calls and texts, store phone numbers, and display the time. It even has caller ID.

>> The DIY Cellphone, which uses the GSM shield hardware and software, includes an LED screen and the ability to store phone numbers, show the time, and identify callers.

EXPLORE THE INTERNET WITH THE ETHERNET SHIELD

More and more people rely on being connected to the Internet for a lot of their day. Enter the Arduino Ethernet shield, which connects an Arduino board to the Internet. Based on an Internet chip called Wiznet W5100, the Ethernet shield can connect to as many as four different socket connections at the same time. It can act as a receiver for incoming connections or a client to make outgoing connections. Users can access Arduino's Ethernet library and, using an Ethernet jack together with the shield, they can write sketches to connect to the Internet.

The most recent version of the Arduino Ethernet includes a micro-SD card slot. This means users now have the option to access and store files they download via the network. Thanks to the handy Ethernet library, this is compatible with both the Uno and Mega boards.

The Ethernet shield can do more than just provide wireless Internet. One user has used it to make his own Web server to host his own Web site. All it takes is an Arduino, the Ethernet shield (make sure it's compatible with the Arduino used for the project), a spare port on a router or switch and a cable, and the sample Web server provided by Arduino.

The Ethernet shield has proved to be quite successful. Adafruit.com lists the Arduino Ethernet shield as one of its top choices for an electronic gift.

PRIME PROTOTYPING

People interested in creating their own unique circuits might give the Arduino Prototyping (Proto) shield a look. Proto is the brainchild of SparkFun Electronics and ITP, the graduate program at Tisch School of the Arts in New York City. The Proto makes it easy to connect Arduino to a breadboard. Users can get right to it by soldering to the prototype area for their own creations. They also have the option of purchasing a separate, small breadboard to test out their ideas without having to solder. When combined with an Arduino development board, the user has use of two basic footprints for LEDs, BlueSMiRF socket access, a place for a basic pushbutton switch, and a reset button at the top level. The BlueSMiRF socket allows for a wireless connection between Arduinos. This shield makes it a snap to make a single unit by combining custom circuits with Arduino.

On its own, the Proto is sometimes called Bare PCB, but users can buy a Proto shield kit, too. In short, the kit has almost all the

>> Some Arduino products, such as the Prototyping (Proto) shield, require the user to know how to do a bit of soldering, which the student in this photo is practicing.

hardware the user needs to get started with this shield. The kit doesn't come with a breadboard, but many users highly recommend it. The user is responsible for soldering the final product.

Arduino offers the Wireless Proto shield, which, as the name suggests, makes it possible for an Arduino board to communicate wirelessly using a wireless module. It can communicate at up to 100 feet (31 meters) indoors and 300 feet (91 meters) outdoors.

ACCESSORIES

An accessory is there when we want to make a product more useful, adaptable, or attractive. Arduino has its share of accessories, including a special screen users can draw on and a USB adapter.

DIGITAL DRAWINGS ON THE TFT LCD SCREEN

The Arduino TFT screen lets users draw almost whatever they want—words or pictures—on a backlit screen. The TFT LCD screen uses the TFT library, which is based in part on the Adafruit library. Users can use it to do other cool things like play games. It has a micro-SD card for saving things such as bitmap images to show on the screen. The screen is compatible with many Arduinos, although users may have to do a little wiring to make that happen. It's ready to fit into sockets of the Arduino Esplora and Robot.

USB/SERIAL LIGHT ADAPTER

The USB/Serial Light Adapter is what's used to convert a USB to a microcontroller module like the Arduino Mini or Ethernet so that it can talk to a computer. It doesn't even need an external

>>BUST OUT THE BREAKOUT BOARDS

Newer integrated circuits (ICs), sensors, and drivers are available with small surface mounts, making it tricky to access those tiny pins. These smaller setups do not plug directly into the larger breadboards or the pins might not fit the breadboard. Hello, breakout board. A breakout board, also known as a printed circuit board (PCB), is a lot like a breadboard, but it requires some soldering work to keep all connections. If the user is making a rapid prototype, the breakout board could save her or him a lot of time. Breakout boards might also come with other handy parts like larger screws.

Breakout boards come in many different patterns for all sorts of projects, but if the preprinted boards don't work for a certain project, don't fret. Inexpensive adapters can plug right into a basic breadboard. If one of these is needed, some users suggest double-checking with the company to make sure it's in stock before ordering. Otherwise, the project might have to wait a few weeks for the adapter to arrive. If all else fails, it's possible to have a custom board printed out by a PCB company.

driver. The adapter connects to the Arduino Ethernet, Mini, Pro Mini, LilyPad, LilyPad Simple, and Fio. (Boards like the Uno, Duemilanove, Diecimila, Nano, and Mega already have a chip to do this.) The Mini USB adapter connects to microcontrollers, like the Arduino Mini.

>> The Arduino starter kit is a great way for the beginner to get going because it includes instructions for a few different projects and many parts.

INSIDE THE ARDUINO STARTER KIT

A good place to start using Arduino might be with the starter kit. Users who want some extra help with setting up an Arduino sometimes consider this kit. It includes instructions for several projects as well as many of the parts needed. Open up the box and here's what's inside version 3.0 of the starter kit:

- Arduino Uno
- USB cable
- 9V battery pack w/DC plug (requires soldering)
- A clear breadboard
- Deluxe jumper wires
- Assorted LEDs
- Assorted resistors
- Two "momentary buttons"

OK, now what? Start playing! Projects users can make with the starter kit include Light Theremin, a musical instrument played with the hands; Spaceship Interface, a control panel for a spaceship; Touchy-Feel Lamp, a lamp that responds to touch; and Zoetrope, a way to create mechanical animation that moves forward and backward. Once the user has a sense of what Arduino can do and how to do it, it's time to start making his or her own projects, or as the Arduino Web site says, "Build it, hack it and share it. Because Arduino is you!"

ADDITIVE MANUFACTURING Making things one layer at a time based on a three-dimensional design.

ANALOG Information represented by a constantly changing characteristic of electrical current, as opposed to digital.

CLOCK SPEED The speed at which a computer or its micro-processor operates (how fast it performs internal operations expressed in cycles per second, or megahertz).

EEPROM Memory whose values are kept when the board is turned off (like a tiny hard drive).

FTDI CABLE A USB to serial (TTL level) converter, which allows for a simple way to connect TTL interface devices to a USB.

GENERAL PACKET RATING SERVICE (GPRS) Helps mobile users access the Internet for e-mail and Web browsing over the telephone network.

INTEGRATED CIRCUIT An electronic circuit made on a small piece of semiconducting material that does the same thing as a larger circuit made from discrete components.

INTEGRATED DEVELOPMENT ENVIRONMENT (IDE) An all-in-one piece of software that allows users to write and run programs.

JUMPER A short wire used to connect an electric circuit or sidestep a break in a circuit.

OPEN SOURCE Term used for software for which the original source code is free and open to be modified and redistributed.

PLATFORM The requirement for what kinds of software a computer can run.

PROTOTYPE The first model of something, from which other models are developed.

PWM (PULSE-WIDTH MODULATION) A digital wave with a constant frequency, but the tiny bit of time when the signal is on can be varied.

RAPID PROTOTYPE The quick creation of a new model.

SERIAL A connection in a computer system when information is conducted over a single wire.

SIM CARD Short for subscriber identification module; the smart card in a cell phone that carries a unique identification number that prevents its operation if removed.

SOLDER To melt a metal with a low melting point, such as lead or tin, in order to join two metals that have a high melting point.

SYSTEM An arrangement in which all units assemble and work together according to a program or plan.

USB (UNIVERSAL SERIAL BUS) A link that allows simplified attachment of disks, modems, printers, and more to a computer without special software or having to reboot the computer.

VOLTAGE An electrical force or potential difference expressed in volts.

Association of Information Technology Professionals (AITP)
330 N. Wabash Avenue, Suite 2000
Chicago, IL 60611
(800) 224-9371
(312) 245-1070
Web site: http://www.aitp.org
The Association of Information Technology Professionals, which
has gone by other names since its start in 1951, strives to
advance the information technology profession through
professional development, education, and more.

Canadian Computer Society
260 Adelaide Street East, #210
Toronto, ON M5A 1N1
Canada
(416) 299-5282
Web site: http://www.cancomputes.com
The Canadian Computer Society offers information, conducts
research, and promotes study in all areas of computer
technology.

Geek Girl
3539 Curtis Street
San Diego, CA 92106
(866) 933-3218
(774) 269-9222
Web site: http://geekgirlcamp.com

Women and young women with beginner, intermediate, and advanced computer skills can find technology conferences, workshops, and seminars through the Geek Girl network.

Girls Who Code
28 West 23rd Street, 4th Floor
New York, NY 10010
Web site: http://www.girlswhocode.com
In 2012, Girls Who Code launched a national nonprofit organization to teach, motivate, and prepare high school girls interested in computing.

HackerYou
The Centre for Social Innovation - Annex
720 Bathurst Street, Suite 500
Toronto, ON M5S 2R4
Canada
Web site: http://www.hackeryou.com
Anyone who wants to learn coding will find information, as well as hands-on classes and workshops, through HackerYou.

Iridescent
532 West 22nd Street
New York, NY 10011
(718) 502-9555
Web site: http://iridescentlearning.org

Iridescent is a nonprofit organization that uses science, technology, and engineering to prove that knowledge is empowering. It particularly seeks to pique the curiosity of school girls and underprivileged minority children and their families.

National Association of Programmers
P.O. Box 529
Prairieville, LA 70769
Web site: http://www.napusa.org
Formed in 1995, the National Association of Programmers provides information and resources for programmers, developers, consultants, and other professionals and students in the computer industry.

National Center for Women & Information Technology (NCWIT)
University of Colorado
Campus Box 322 UCB
Boulder, CO 80309-0322
(303) 735-6671
Web site: http://www.ncwit.org
The NCWIT is a nonprofit organization offering "community, evidence, and action" for women who want a place in the world of technology.

Open Source Initiative (OSI)
855 El Camino Real
Ste 13A, #270

Palo Alto, CA 94301

Web site: http://opensource.org

The Open Source Initiative manages the open-source definition and is responsible of reviewing and approving open-source definition licenses. The OSI builds communities, educates, and promotes public advocacy of the awareness of open-source software.

WEB SITES

Due to the changing nature of Internet links, Rosen Publishing has developed an online list of Web sites related to the subject of this book. This site is updated regularly. Please use this link to access the list:

http://www.rosenlinks.com/CODE/Ardu

{FOR FURTHER READING

Baichtal, John, Matthew Beckler, and Adam Wolf. *Make: LEGO and Arduino Projects*. Sebastopol, CA: Maker Media, 2013.

Banzi, Massimo. *Getting Started with Arduino*. 2nd ed. Sebastopol, CA: Maker Media, 2011.

Bell, Charles. *Beginning Sensor Networks with Arduino and Raspberry Pi*. Berkeley, CA: Apress, 2013.

Blum, Jeremy. *Exploring Arduino Tools and Techniques for Engineering Wizardry*. Indianapolis, IN: John Wiley & Sons, 2013.

Borenstein, Greg. *Making Things See: 3D Vision with Kinect, Processing, Arduino, and MakerBot*. Sebastopol, CA: Maker Media, 2012.

Boxall, John. *Arduino Workshop*. Sebastopol, CA: O'Reilly Media, 2013.

Craft, Brock. *Arduino Projects for Dummies*. Chichester, England: John Wiley & Sons, 2013.

Igoe, Tom. *Making Things Talk*. Sebastopol, CA: Maker Media, 2011.

LEAD Project. *Super Scratch Programming Adventure! Learn to Program by Making Cool Games*. San Francisco, CA: No Starch Press, 2012.

Margolis, Michael. *Make an Arduino-Controlled Robot*. Sebastopol, CA: O'Reilly Media, 2012.

McComb, Gordon. *Arduino Robot Bonanza*. New York, NY: McGraw-Hill, 2013.

McComb, Gordon. *Robot Builder's Bonanza*. New York, NY: McGraw-Hill, 2011.

Melgar, Enrique Ramos, and Ciriaco Castro Diez. *Arduino and Kinect Projects: Design, Build, Blow Their Minds*. Berkeley, CA: Apress, 2012.

Monk, Simon. *15 Dangerously Mad Projects for the Evil Genius*. New York, NY: McGraw-Hill, 2011.

Monk, Simon. *30 Arduino Projects for the Evil Genius*. New York, NY: McGraw-Hill, 2013.

Nussey, John. *Arduino for Dummies*. Chichester, England: John Wiley & Sons, 2013.

Pakhchyan, Syuzi. *Fashioning Technology: A DIY Intro to Smart Crafting*. Sebastopol, CA: O'Reilly Media, 2013.

Sande, Warren, and Carter Sande. *Hello World! Computer Programming for Kids and Other Beginners*. Greenwich, CT: Manning Publications, 2013.

Williams, Josh, and Terence O'Neill. *Arduino*. Ann Arbor, MI: Cherry Lake Publishing, 2013.

{BIBLIOGRAPHY

Alaejos, Raúl, and Rodrigo Calvo, directors. "Arduino: The Documentary." 2011. Retrieved August 27, 2013 (http://arduinothedocumentary.org).

Arduino. Retrieved August 27, 2013 (http://www.arduino.cc).

Boysen, Earl, and Nancy C. Muir. "Electronics Basics: Using a Breadboard." Retrieved August 27, 2013 (http://www.dummies.com/how-to/content/electronics-basics-using-a-breadboard.html).

Engineers Garage. "What Is an Embedded System?" Retrieved July 20, 2013 (http://www.engineersgarage.com/articles/embedded-systems).

Forefront.io. "The Absolute Beginner's Guide to Arduino." Retrieved August 27, 2013 (http://forefront.io/a/beginners-guide-to-arduino).

Karvinen, Kimmo, and Tero Karvinen. *Make: Arduino Bots and Gadgets*. Sebastopol, CA: O'Reilly Media, 2011.

Ladyada. "Arduino Uno FAQ," Retrieved August 27, 2013 (http://learn.adafruit.com/arduino-tips-tricks-and-techniques/arduino-uno-faq).

LaHart, Justin. "Taking an Open-Source Approach to Hardware." *Wall Street Journal*. Retrieved August 27, 2013 (http://online.wsj.com/article/SB10001424052748703499404574559960271468066.html).

MakeUseOf.com. "What Is Arduino and What Can You Do with It?" Retrieved August 27, 2013 (http://www.makeuseof.com/tag/arduino-technology-explained).

Margolis, Michael. *Arduino Cookbook*. Sebastopol, CA: O'Reilly Media, 2012.

Monk, Simon. *Hacking Electronics: An Illustrated DIY Guide for Makers and Hobbyists*. New York, NY: McGraw-Hill, 2013.

Monk, Simon. *Programming Arduino: Getting Started with Sketches*. New York, NY: McGraw-Hill, 2012.

Olsson, Tony. *Arduino Wearables*. New York, NY: Apress, 2012.

Schmidt, Maik. *Arduino: A Quick-Start Guide*. Dallas, TX: The Pragmatic Bookshelf, 2011.

SparkFun. "ProtoShield Quickstart Guide." Retrieved August 27, 2013 (https://www.sparkfun.com/tutorials/191).

ABOUT THE AUTHOR

Heather Moore Niver is a New York State author and editor. She has participated in juried poetry workshops at the New York State Writer's Institute and the Edna St. Vincent Millay Society, and every winter she leads a writing workshop at an Adirondack arts retreat. She has written more than twenty nonfiction young adult books about everything from anglerfish to skydiving.

PHOTO CREDITS